A Miracle Named Angel

Karen Leite

Karen Leite

AuthorHouse™
1663 Liberty Drive, Suite 200
Bloomington, IN 47403
www.authorhouse.com
Phone: 1-800-839-8640

© 2009 Karen Leite. All rights reserved.

No part of this book may be reproduced, stored in a retrieval system, or transmitted by any means without the written permission of the author.

First published by AuthorHouse 2/5/2009

ISBN: 978-1-4389-5246-8 (sc)

Library of Congress Control Number: 2009900710

Printed in the United States of America
Bloomington, Indiana

This book is printed on acid-free paper.

Dedicated to my husband Antonio.
Without his help Angel would not be alive.

Thanks to my sons,
Kevin and Brian, and
my nephews, Jeffrey and Gregory.
They were the first to notice that Angel
was about to be born.

Also special thanks to
my mom, Marge,
my sister, Lori, and brother-in-law, Jeff,
and my friend Marty,
for all their work during the birth of Angel.

A baby goat was born on a Friday in spring,

He was a few weeks early, so no one expected a thing.

The baby looked healthy; we were all so very glad.

Then in a little while, we were worried and sad.

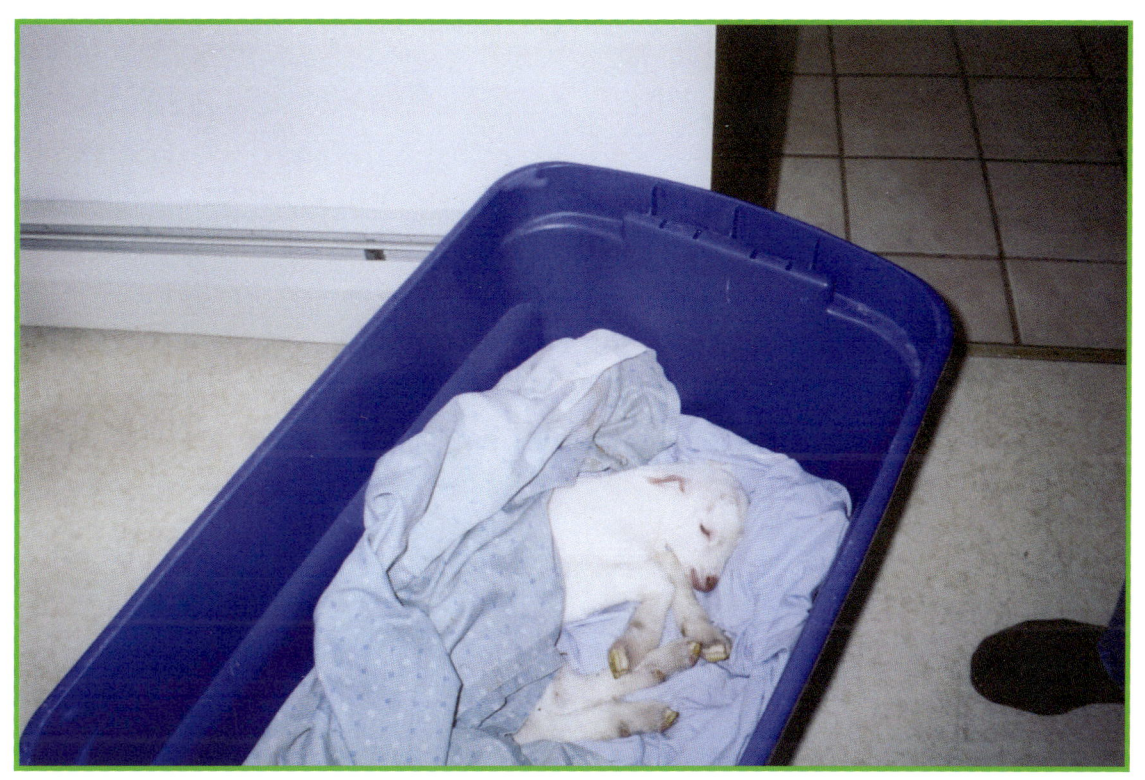

His hair was all white, and it felt just like silk,

But he couldn't stand up to drink his mom's milk.

He was so weak that we thought he would die,

We wanted to save him; we just had to try.

We took the baby from his mom and brought him inside.

It was so cold that night, we were sure he would have died.

We had to keep him warm with a special heating light.

We took milk from his mom MJ, and fed him through the night.

We asked a few people how to help him survive.

We loved that little goat; we just had to keep him alive.

My family and I prayed every day, it is true,

And I felt that God told me what I had to do.

We gave him extra milk, nice and warm, but not hot,

And I held him in my arms and rubbed him a lot.

On Tuesday the baby had made it to day four.

After my husband, Antonio, worked with him, he stood up on the floor.

We took him to his mom so she would know he was okay,

And I thought of a name for him the very next day.

I thought he was our miracle sent for my family to love,

So I named him Angel, the goat sent from Heaven above.

He was getting so much better,

And he was as happy as could be.

He stayed outside during the day with mom,

And at night he came in the house with me.

My sons, Kevin and Brian, liked to play with Angel and his mother.

Soon they started to call him their new baby brother.

On Friday I brought Angel to Tinker School for the day,

After the principal said it was okay.

The children were excited; he was such a great surprise.

Everybody loved Angel; you could see it in their eyes.

On Sunday we visited the Alzheimer's Center

To see my dad, Gus, for a while.

Angel came with us and made the people

Who live and work there smile.

On Tuesday Antonio brought Angel to James Morris School

To see Kevin and Brian, which was against the rule.

But Angel was such a big hit.

He made the children laugh and play.

The teachers didn't say a thing

When they saw the goat that day.

Now that it is warmer,

He will stay in the barn at night.

He is so much stronger now,

We know he'll be all right.

I believe Angel was put here

For lots of people to enjoy.

I'm so glad that MJ is willing

To share her little boy.

I would like to thank God, up in Heaven above,

For sending cute little Angel for all of us to love.

About the Author

Karen Leite has been a teacher for over twenty years and is currently teaching Kindergarten. She resides in Lakeside with her husband and 2 sons.

Printed in the United States
138199LV00003B